HEALTH CHOICES

RELATIONSHIPS

Cath Senker

HODDER
Wayland

An imprint of Hodder Children's Books

Text copyright © Cath Senker 2004

Consultant: Jayne Wright
Design: Sarah Borny

Published in Great Britain in 2004
by Hodder Wayland, an imprint of
Hodder Children's Books

The publishers would like to thank the following for allowing
us to reproduce their pictures in this book:
Hodder Wayland Picture Library; 4, 5, 6, 7, 8, 9, 10, 11, 13, 14
15, 16, 17, 18, 19, 20, 21 / Zul Mukhida; 12

A catalogue record for this book is available from the British Library.

ISBN 07502 45034

Printed in China by WKT

Hodder Children's Books
A division of Hodder Headline Limited
338 Euston Road, London NW1 3BH

Contents

What kinds of family are there?

There are lots of different kinds! Many kids live with Mum and Dad. Sadly, sometimes mums and dads don't get on any more. They may decide to live in different homes.

Maybe your mum or dad lives with somebody else now. Perhaps you live with different people too. You might have a **stepmother** or stepfather, or stepsisters and stepbrothers.

Perhaps you live just with

Mum or just with Dad

or even Gran and

Grandad.

Sometimes

other *carers* look

after kids. All families

have some things in common.

They are people who live together

and try to care for each other.

How many different kinds of family do you know? What's the same and what's different about how they live?

Why do I have to share my things?

Sharing is kind. If you share, it shows you care.

It means you are thinking about other people.

It's a friendly thing to do.

People will like you

and want to

play with you

if you share

your things

with them.

Which things can you share with your brother, sister or friend? Which things can't you share, and why?

Do you ever feel **jealous**? You might be jealous of your brother or sister. Perhaps they were given fantastic new toys for their birthday, and you want to play with them.

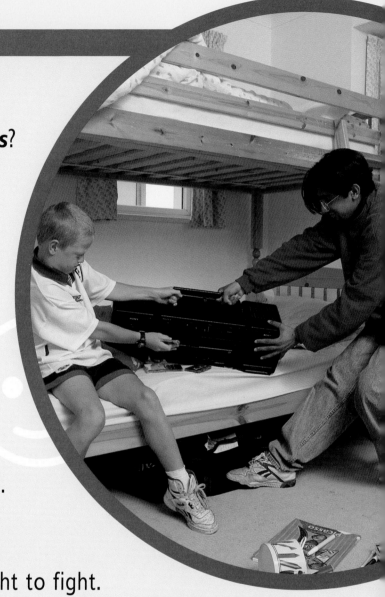

Remember – it's not right to fight.

If you share your toys, others will share their toys with you. When you share your things, you can have more fun together.

Why do I have to tidy up?

 Tidying up is helpful. As you grow older, you can do more things for yourself. You can tidy your own room, and help with the washing up. You can care for pets.

Smaller children or elderly people might like your help too. Helping people is very grown up and makes you feel good.

If you help other people, they'll be happier to help you. Just think – if you help Dad to wash the car he'll have more time to play a game with you or read a story.

How do you help at home? Who helps you each day?

Why do I have to listen?

'Pick up the phone! Leave that alone!' Adults often have to tell you important things. They may need your help. Sometimes they might call to warn you about *danger*.

It's horrible when people don't listen to you. It makes you feel small and not important. You don't want to make other people feel like that, do you? Take turns to listen and talk. You'll find out interesting things and hear some new ideas.

Can you think of a time when you didn't listen and something bad happened?

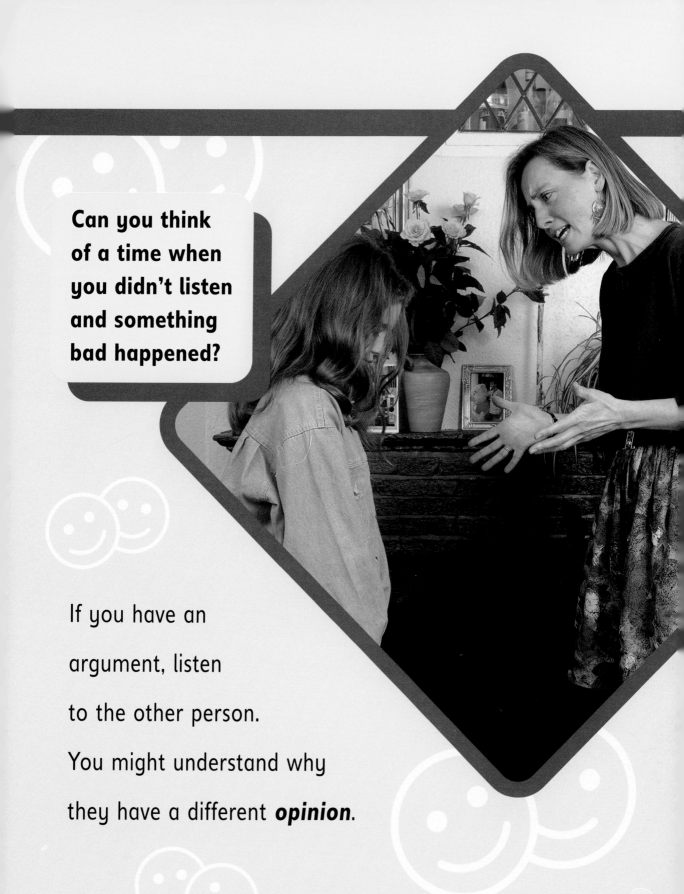

If you have an

argument, listen

to the other person.

You might understand why

they have a different *opinion*.

Why are we moving house?

There are many reasons for moving house. Perhaps a parent has a new job in a different place. You might be moving to a home with a bit more space.

You may have to go to a new school and get to know new people. You might feel shy – it's easy to see why. You will cope with the change and you will learn to become more **confident.**

It might take a bit of time. Don't worry – you will soon settle in and make new friends.

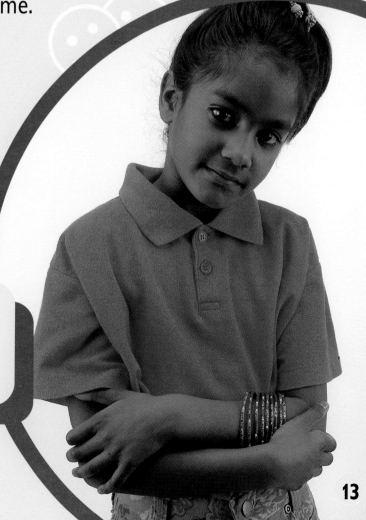

Have you ever moved to a new place? What did it feel like?

13

How can I help the new boy?

Talk to him and get to know him! It's good to get to know new people. They probably know some exciting games or interesting things.

At break time, be kind – don't leave him behind! You can show the new boy around the school. Why not ask him to join in your game? At lunchtime you can invite him to sit with you and your friends.

Think about how you would feel if it was your first day. What would you like others to do to make you feel welcome and comfortable?

Say, 'What's your name? Want to join our game?'

Have you had a new child in your class and how did you welcome him or her?

Why do other kids pick on me?

Some children hurt other children or make them feel sad on purpose. They are **bullies**. Bullies hurt others because it makes them feel 'big'. Perhaps they have their own problems to sort out.

How do you think it feels to be bullied?

Teachers need to know if children keep upsetting or hurting you. They will talk to the bullies and help them to understand why it is wrong to hurt other kids.

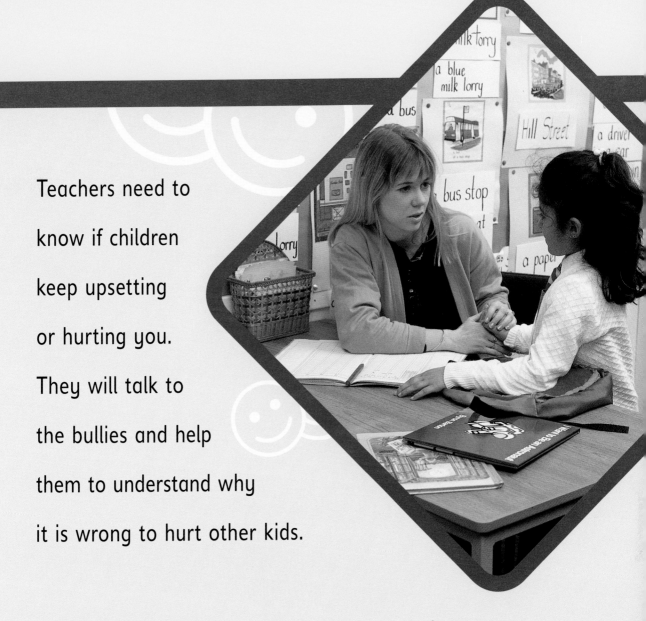

It is important to tell an adult if you are being picked on. Bullies pick on all sorts of children, for many different reasons. Remember – it is not your fault if you have done nothing to annoy them.

Why did grandpa die?

When people grow very old they die. Occasionally they die younger because they are ill or have an accident.

When someone dies, it is normal to feel very sad. You might even feel angry with them for dying because they are not there for you any more. It's fine to show you are unhappy.

It's better to talk about it than to keep quiet and be miserable inside.

You might want to look at photos of the person to remember them.

Do you know anyone who has died, or have you had a pet that died? How do you feel now?

What can I do when I feel sad?

 Everyone feels sad sometimes. If you are sad because of a problem, it's good to talk to your friends or family. It's fine to cry and let out your feelings.

Try to find things to do that make you feel better. Spending some time on your own may help. You could do a drawing or painting to show how you feel inside.

How about listening to your favourite music or watching a video? Doing sport is great too. Running around releases **chemicals** in your body that make you feel happier.

Glossary and index

Finding out more

Books to read:

Don't Do That!
by Janine Amos
(Cherrytree Books, 2003)

Don't Say That!
by Janine Amos
(Cherrytree Books, 2003)

Go Away!
by Janine Amos
(Cherrytree Books, 2003)

It's Mine!
by Janine Amos
(Cherrytree Books, 2003)

It Won't Work!
by Janine Amos
(Cherrytree Books, 2003)

Move Over!
by Janine Amos
(Cherrytree Books, 2003)

Why Should I Help?
by Claire Llewellyn
and Mike Gordon
(Hodder Wayland, 2001)

Why Should I Listen?
by Claire Llewellyn
and Mike Gordon
(Hodder Wayland, 2001)

Why Should I Share?
by Claire Llewellyn
and Mike Gordon
(Hodder Wayland, 2001)